Poetry?
But i don't do poetry!

Sharon George

Poetry? But I Don't Do Poetry!

ISBN 978-1-907929-93-9

Front Cover: Claire Hartley and Bethany George
Illustrations: Rob Griffiths
CD Recordings: Sharon George and Stuart Bell
CD Music: Clare Bell

Lp

Editing, design and layout by Life Publications
www.lifepublications.org.uk

Recommendations

It is a pleasure for me to recommend this book highly to you. Sharon attended our internship *'Closer'* here at *Living Stones House of Prayer Cyprus* back in 2014. Sharon is a larger than life personality with a wonderful sense of humour. It was a beautiful work of God that took place in her life during her time with us.

Struggling with comprehension her whole life, she was faced with her own limitations and disappointments in our classroom setting. But instead of experiencing defeat once again, she had an incredible breakthrough that led her to be able to articulate herself in a way that was edifying for us all. The gift that God has released in Sharon's life is a gift for His people.

As you read her story be encouraged that it's never too late for God to do something new and creative in your life to be a source of blessing to many.

Martin Dolan
Director, Living Stones House of Prayer Cyprus

A fundamental truth of the cross is stated in Colossians 3:3-4,

> *For you have died and your life is hidden with Christ in God. When Christ, who is our life, is revealed, then you also will be revealed with Him in glory.*

It is a beautiful and wonderful thing when Jesus reveals His life and glory through a person. When we saw how the Holy Spirit birthed this beautiful and powerful gift of anointed poetry in Sharon, and especially after she told us about her difficulties in English from childhood, we were in complete awe of the Lord's kindness and power, and we thoroughly rejoiced in how Jesus was and is honouring Sharon and her love for Him through the poems He continues to give her.

We trust and pray that those reading this book and especially the poems will similarly worship Jesus for His goodness and power in this miraculous gift, but even more that you would be touched and changed by the power of the revelatory truths of Christ and His love amazingly captured in Sharon's poems. We pray that you also would encounter Him in wonderful life-changing ways and that your walk with Jesus would become as a result, much, much closer.

Stephen & Angela Boler
School of Prophetic Ministry

Acknowledgements

I would like to say thank you to my husband, Lloyd George, and daughter, Bethany George, who have encouraged and supported me throughout the writing of this book.

I would like to say thank you to Martin and Heike Dolan and Stephen and Angela Boler who journeyed with me through the beginning of this testimony, for their love, teaching and support and for encouraging me to write this book.

I would like to say thank you to all those who read and reread and then read this book again and helped to steer me to write this finished version; too many to name individually but mainly Rhiannon Thomas and Janice Bell – bless you.

I would like to say a big thank you to Clare Bell, Stuart Bell, Rob Griffiths, Claire Hartley and Bethany George for their creative input. Thanks guys, it looks and sounds great!

I would like to say my biggest thank you to my Abba Father, without whom this book would not be written. It's solely because of you Lord, that I have this testimony to share. Thank You.

Poetry? But I Don't Do Poetry!

Poetry?
But I Don't Do Poetry!

Poetry? But I Don't Do Poetry!

Preface

When I was eight years old, I moved to a new school, and after a couple of weeks my teacher called my mother in to have a word with her. As I stood next to my mother in the classroom the teacher explained to her that in the subject of English, my level was very poor. The teacher went on to say that I was way behind with my reading, writing and comprehension skills and would always struggle in this area.

The power of words spoken over us, both good and bad, are capable of having a major impact on our lives.

When we are told something and we fully believe and receive those words, whether they are a lie or the truth, those words can become deeply embedded within us. I truly believed all my life that I had a major problem with comprehension. It didn't matter how many times people told me that it wasn't true; I simply didn't believe them, as I always referred back to the deeply embedded words spoken into me that I thought were the real truth.

I could read just fine, but I often did not understand what I was reading nor understand the meaning of the words. When reading a book, as soon as I came across a word that I didn't understand or a sentence that just didn't make sense to me, I would become frustrated and would give up. This usually occurred by about the end of the second page! In the end I just stopped trying. I gave up on the idea of reading as it was not for me, therefore I never really read any books at all.

I became a Christian when I was 24 years old and I did try and read the Bible, but I could not understand it at all. My Bible was full of thees, thous, shalts and wilts and I could not figure out whether the words were referring to me, God or someone else entirely. I got very confused and so gave up trying. Consequently, I rarely picked up the Bible, after all it was a book, and I didn't do books.

Eventually, about 15 years after becoming a Christian, I shared this problem with a friend. I showed him my Bible and after raising his eyebrows and saying very little, he sent me off to the Christian Book Shop with instructions to purchase a different version and to return to him with it. I did not know you could get different versions of the Bible, such was my disinterest in books. He showed me how to read the Bible in a different way and how I could hear the voice of God through reading it. I was in awe when, for the first time, I heard God speak to me as I read. I still struggled with comprehension though, and I still did not like books so I still did not read the Bible very much at all, I just dipped in to it now and then, which was an improvement but still not as it should have been.

This continued for another five years or so. After a lifetime of a fear of big words and being unable to comprehend them, I was absolutely convinced that I had a major problem in the ability to read and comprehend and just accepted that, it did not occur to me to try and do something about it. I still didn't like books, so I guess I just wasn't that bothered. I thought books were pretty boring, they held no interest for me.

I had absolutely no idea that God was going to change all this so profoundly. This book shares the testimony of how God creatively used poetry to break through the lie I was believing, how God taught, encouraged and comforted me through poetry and gave me revelation through this that I was now free to read the Bible.

Poetry? But I don't do Poetry!

*H*ave you ever found yourself having a gentle discussion with the Holy Spirit which kind of implies that He may have made a mistake? Okay, so I was having a slight disagreement with the Holy Spirit! Let me take you back a little step here so that I can explain to you what led to this particular disagreement and rather one-sided conversation.

Back in the beginning of 2014, through a series of God encounters, dreams, visions and prophetic words, God very clearly asked me to finish my job and go to Cyprus for six weeks on an Internship called *Closer*. The internship focused on your relationship with God and drawing closer to Him and was led by Martin and Heike Dolan in their House of Prayer called *Living Stones* situated in Kiti near Larnaca.

The Internship ran for six weeks during October and November of that year. So, I signed up, quit my job and off I went, very excited.

As part of the course, the team planned to hold a non-stop 24-hour worship event and invited every intern to sign up to lead a one-hour slot and gave permission for us to do whatever we wanted to during those sessions. So, I knew this was coming up, and had already thought about it, and had decided that the easiest thing for me to do was to simply lead an hour of good old Christian worship choruses via YouTube – nice and easy.

On the Monday morning, the fourth week of the internship, we were given a sign-up sheet so that we could choose a slot and write our names against the time. I wasn't expecting it, but there was another box next to it in which we needed to write what we were going to do for that hour, and I went to write "YouTube worship" and then hesitated as I remembered all that we had been learning over the past three weeks, and so I paused just long enough to quickly ask God what He wanted me to do. I wasn't really expecting a response, as I already had the answer, and was therefore somewhat taken aback when He answered me, not only very clearly but with an answer that I was just totally unprepared for. The conversation went something like this:

Sharon: Father, what do you want me to do for this hour of worship?

Holy Spirit: Poetry.

Sharon: Poetry?

Holy Spirit: Poetry.

Poetry? But I Don't Do Poetry!

Sharon:	But I don't do poetry!
Holy Spirit:	(Silence)
Sharon:	What am I supposed to do with that?
Holy Spirit:	(More silence)
Sharon:	But I don't even *like* poetry, it's boring.
Holy Spirit:	(Still silent)
Sharon:	Wouldn't you rather an hour of good old Christian worship choruses? The old ones are really great. They really exalt your name.
Holy Spirit:	(Putting into practice the fine art of being patiently silent)
Sharon:	Poetry?
Holy Spirit:	Poetry.
Sharon:	OKAY, I will write poetry in the time slot, though what YOU are going to do about that I do not know.

So, I wrote "Poetry" in the slot in complete obedience but also in complete lack of faith and walked off mumbling to myself.

I could never have foreseen what God was about to do in me and through me that very evening.

Poetry? But I Don't Do Poetry!

1

What Does the Finished Work of the Cross Mean to Me?

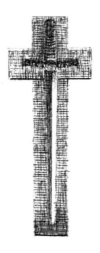

*L*ater that same day, Stephen and Angela, our teachers, set us some homework and the homework was that everyone was to write a poem, a song or a creative piece of writing based on the previous week's teaching, to include the areas we had been impacted in by the Holy Spirit.

In order for me to fully share this testimony and for you to understand why this homework put me into a panic, I need to take you back to the beginning of the previous week.

For weeks three and four of the internship, Martin and Heike had invited Stephen and Angela Boler, a lovely couple extremely gifted in teaching and the prophetic, to come and teach us on "The Cross" for the first week and "Praise, Prayer and Prophecy" for the second week.

The first two weeks of the internship had been absolutely amazing, and I was learning so much and loving every minute of it. My knowledge of, and relationship with God was growing and I was hearing His voice so much more clearly. So, I was extremely excited for what Stephen and Angela were going to bring.

During their introduction, Stephen and Angela shared with us that they had been studying the finished work of the cross for about 40 years and were here to share with us what they had learned and discovered on their journey. I was really looking forward to this teaching, but for some reason I began to feel unsettled and nervous.

Just before I go fully into this testimony, I would like to make it very clear that this testimony is in no way a negative reflection on the teaching given by Stephen and Angela; their teaching was excellent, it is all about what was going on within my own head and whose voice I was listening to.

So on with the story …

As Stephen led the first session that afternoon, that old deeply embedded lie within me (that I believed to be truth) began to rear its ugly head. All I was hearing internally was, "Sharon, this is not for you. You won't understand this. There is no point in listening. You are not intelligent enough for this. Go home."

I tried to fight this onslaught of negative words because I really wanted to listen and learn, and so I tried to get past them, but they just kept going around and round in my head, taking over as they did so. The biggest problem I had was that I actually believed these words I was listening to; I didn't see them as lies. As the negative words swirled around in my head, fear and panic began to rise and as the session went on, negativity became the dominant focus.

By the time I got back to our lodging house that evening, internally I was in a terrible emotional state. I had convinced myself that I was not bright enough for this, and therefore didn't know how I was going to cope with the rest of the week. I had totally lost my peace and felt like packing up and going home. I ended up with a nasty headache and felt like I was under extreme pressure. Though I shared a little with my housemates and they prayed for me, I was actually too embarrassed to tell them the whole truth of what was really going on.

I went to bed exhausted, with this fierce battle still raging on the inside. I resigned myself to not being fully capable of understanding, but I also decided that I would give it my best. I quite simply said to the Holy Spirit, "You are my teacher, help me to grasp what I need to grasp and not to worry about everything else. If you need me to get this then you will have to help me because I cannot do this."

And so, the week and the teaching continued. Stephen and Angela took it in turns to lead the sessions and though I still struggled with lots of negative thoughts swirling around my head, I tried to remain focused on what I knew I had understood and just ignored everything else. By choosing to listen well, choosing not to worry and choosing to trust the Holy Spirit, as the week progressed, I felt like I was moving slowly forward. As the week came to an end and I looked back, I believed that whilst I had not understood a large amount of what was taught, I felt my understanding in some areas had grown a little and I was pleased about that. In all honesty I was relieved that I had got through the week and now I could relax.

So, when Angela announced the aforementioned homework to be written based on how we had been impacted by the Holy Spirit in all of the previous week's teaching, there was an explosion of panic inside me, I was emotionally undone, and therefore immediately back to where I had started from the previous Monday. That old embedded truth (lie) resurfaced and took over again. The voice inside my head was saying, "You can't do this Sharon, you didn't understand the teaching, this is impossible for you, give up." I couldn't think for the life of me how on earth I was going to do this homework. I didn't have the answer. I felt that the assignment was going to be way too difficult for me to even attempt. The progress I had made during the previous week seemed to be snatched away in an instant.

That night as I sat in bed with notebook and pen in hand, I wrote down the title of the homework Stephen and Angela had given, as I wanted to pray quickly about it before going to sleep. I wrote down, "What does the finished work of the cross mean to me?" and to my absolute amazement I continued to write … "Jesus secured me a pardon instead of a penalty." Then a third sentence came and then a fourth. I didn't understand what was going on, but words started flowing quickly and easily and I rushed to write them all down. I began to see a poem take shape in front of my very eyes. I couldn't believe it! I worked on the poem until about midnight and I was loving every minute of it.

I was so very excited that I desperately needed to share it with someone, so I went to see if my housemate, Carol, was still awake. After I stuck my head through her bedroom door into the darkness and called out her name very loudly about three times, I found that Carol was in fact awake – amazing! So, I read her my poem, shut her bedroom door and went back to bed very happy indeed.

The next day I didn't have class till the afternoon, so I began to look over the poem, and much to my surprise, again more words started to flow. I had written four verses the night before and during the course of the morning another four verses were added. I knew that this was not me; it was definitely the Holy Spirit at work in me, pulling out all the teaching that I had listened to, drawing information together from that which I believed I hadn't grasped, and putting it together in such a way that I could completely understand it. The poem was impacting me in the most incredible way because through it the Holy Spirit was showing me that I *was* capable of understanding. God was breaking down the lie I had lived with all my life. It was an awesome, miraculous breakthrough and I knew it. I was so full of joy.

I spent a couple of hours writing, editing and shaping the lines of the poem until I felt that it was finished. I believed it covered a lot of what we had been taught the previous week. I read it through many times and each time I found myself encountering the Holy Spirit. It made me weep, it caused me to be still, it made me think, it made me extremely happy; and all I could do was speak out praise and thanks to my God.

By the time I got to the House of Prayer I was bouncing with excitement and ran around like a child telling everyone that I had finished my homework. Angela asked me to read my poem out loud and I can tell you that it came as a complete shock to me when I opened my mouth to read the poem that it came out sounding somewhat like a rap! Yes, I did say rap! In my head I was thinking, here I am, a 45-year-old woman, standing in a classroom of 17 people, microphone in hand, rapping a poem for Christ – well okay then!!!

As I was busy rapping away, I could see Angela out of the corner of my eye sitting quietly listening, just nodding her head ever so slightly at the end of each line. She was clearly listening to every single word.

When I finished reading the poem, I looked up at everyone and was met by a wall of silence, and inside I was like "uh oh, not good, perhaps I have got this all wrong." My thoughts went straight to the old negative default setting. Then Angela spoke and simply said, "Can you read it again please?" So, I did.

When I finished this time, it was like the presence of God filled the room and people were being impacted; they began to speak out prayers from the words of the poem and give thanks to God. People were engaging with God all around me, and I just stood there like a lemon in complete silence looking at everyone; I could not understand what on earth had just happened, or what was going on. Angela felt that each area of the topics that she and Stephen had covered the week before had been summarised in the poem by individual sentences, and she was amazed that that was even possible, as was I.

I spent some time with Stephen and Angela afterwards and shared my testimony with them (as I have just shared with you). They went on to share some truths with me that finally cut every last thread of the lie that I had believed all my life about my inability to comprehend. From that conversation with them, the truth that has stuck with me more than any other, is the fact that when I am reading I simply do not have to understand everything in my head, because as I read the Word it goes into my spirit and what I put in there, the Holy Spirit can pull out. I have found real freedom in this truth.

What Does the Finished Work of the Cross Mean to Me?

With God, it is not about understanding all information in your head, but about the Holy Spirit taking that knowledge and transforming it into revelation in your heart.

So, what does the finished work of the cross mean to me? Read on to discover …

The Finished Work of the Cross

What does the finished work of the cross mean to me?
Jesus secured me a pardon instead of a penalty.
I've been redeemed, I've been set free,
Jesus living in my heart is a reality.

Through the shed blood I've been washed, cleansed, forgiven.
I can now enter in to His throne room in heaven.
The Father looks at me and no sin can He see,
He pours out His love, His grace, His mercy.

As I stand in His presence, He explains the story,
I am His precious child chosen to carry His glory.
The moment "Jesus Christ is Lord" I did confess,
My account was credited with His righteousness.

Because I have been adopted, I am in unity,
Delegated power and authority have been given to me.
He draws me into worship that proclaims Him Lord,
He teaches me scripture that sharpens the sword.

A call on my life to be a Priest,
Looking out for the lost, the lonely, the least.
Heaven's resources are fully open to me,
Sharing the Good News to see others set free.

As I meditate on the cross and His sacrifice behold,
I see many facets, His nature, His character unfold.
I see the Groom who poured His blood, His love out for me,
I am the bride drawn in to that place of intimacy.

What Does the Finished Work of the Cross Mean to Me?

Holy Spirit opened my heart, my eye, my ear.
He fills me completely, releasing peace, removing fear.
He walks with me daily, I don't have to do it on my own,
He whispers God's truth and love to me 'til He calls me home.

An honour to minister to the Lord through the veil torn,
Secure in eternal life through the oath He has sworn.
Freedom to walk in the life that was planned long ago for me,
That is what the finished work of the cross means to me.

Monday 27th and Tuesday 28th October, 2014

Poetry? But I Don't Do Poetry!

2

Behold!

$\mathcal{I}$n the evening of the same day as completing and reading my breakthrough poem, a soaking session was scheduled to be held and I didn't want to miss it, I really loved the soaking sessions and was thoroughly blessed by the many that we got to enjoy throughout the entire course of the internship. Most of our soaking sessions involved simply being still and listening to instrumental music being played live, or on CD, and allowing it to wash over us and to wash away worldly thoughts; this in turn allowed us to switch off to this world and all its demands thus leaving us with a greater ability to focus on Jesus and being able to receive anything He might want to share in that moment. For me personally, soaking is about making time and space just to be still and rest in the presence of God with no agenda.

As one of the interns began to lead the soaking session with piano music, I opted to lie down on the rug and simply allow the worship music to wash over me, it was so relaxing and still. All of a sudden, a word popped into my mind. I wasn't surprised by this word as it had been popping into my head for about a week now on and off, but I didn't know why. The word was "Behold". I kept repeating the word over and over, as I had each time it appeared before, but up until that moment I had never got any further with the word than just that. The word had caught my attention and I could not seem to let it go. Eventually, as a sort of question to myself really, I said, "Behold. Behold. What does that word mean?" I was not expecting such an answer to a question I hadn't intentionally asked God, but the Holy Spirit seemed to be whispering in response, "Look and look again at what is yet to be seen."

That rhymes – poem, POEM, *POEM!* Woohoo, I was so excited that I got up, ran over to my bag, grabbed pen and paper and ran back to the rug and began to write down the two lines. The full poem came quickly, not quite a direct dictation from the Holy Spirit, but there was very little effort on my part. The whole poem was penned in about 40 minutes.

At the end of the soaking session I read the poem out to those present, and after I finished reading, the intern, who had been playing the piano, immediately responded, "That's for me, it answers exactly what I have been praying about today with Angela." She was jumping up and down for joy at the way God had just spoken to her and I was so excited to witness this. I felt truly blessed to be used by God in that way.

Behold! So, what does that word mean? Read on to discover what I learned …

Behold!

Behold, behold, what does this word mean?
Look and look again at what is yet to be seen.
Take the time to stop and stare,
Keep looking until you see what is hidden there.
Examine every angle, every twist and turn,
Allow that image in your heart to burn.
Follow every arc, dash, circle and line,
Run with them to see how they all entwine.
Peel back the layers, keep looking deep,
The more you look, the more you reap.
Consider the colours, the shades, what they represent,
The way they flow together, ponder on what is meant.
When you think you have seen all, no more to discover,
Then start all over again, there is so much more to uncover.
Re-fix your gaze in meditation,
And you will receive fresh revelation.
If you apply this teaching to the very last line,
Do it again and again, and take your time,
Your life will be transformed, you will never be the same,
Behold, Behold, the Lamb who was slain.

Tuesday 28th October, 2014

Poetry? But I Don't Do Poetry!

3

Closer

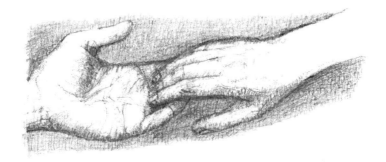

*W*hen I woke up the following day, the words for another poem were flowing straight away. I knew the poem was called *"Closer"* which was not only the name of the Internship we were on, but it was also the very word I had cried out to God back in the beginning of 2014 when I was lying prostrate in God's presence one morning at home.

I quickly wrote down the words I had, and then had to leave it, as it was time to go to the House of Prayer for the day's teaching.

Later that night I found some time and sat down again with the words I had written that morning. I began to work on the poem, with the help of the Holy Spirit, and realised that it was important to use the word "closer" in every verse. The words of the poem were drawn from my experiences with God throughout that year, including the internship, and from the invitation that He had given me and my response to Him.

I really do believe that the cry of "closer" coming out from deep within my heart at the beginning of that year was the moment from where this journey began for me, which is why this poem means so much, it still affects me now, even four years further on in my journey.

It is still my heart's cry: *CLOSER* …

Closer

The invitation is given, come closer my child,
I mull this over, think about it for a while.
What is He asking, what must I do?
I consider the cost to my life over choosing you.

Then I remember your cost, your sacrificed son,
No longer do my wants matter, the deal is done.
I surrender my life, to that I choose to die,
Closer, closer, is my heart's cry.

The closer I come, the closer He comes,
I only walk, but the Father He runs.
I look to Him, to me He turns His face,
And opens His arms for a loving embrace.

I encounter love from the Father, and love from the Son,
I engage with the Spirit, we partner as one.
He draws me closer and willingly I go,
I see His wounds, His sacrifice I know.

I look where I'm at now, and I'm dissatisfied,
There must be more than this, for me Christ died.
I cry out to the Father, "God what is your will?"
"My child", He whispers, "come closer still".

Wednesday 29th October, 2014

Poetry? But I Don't Do Poetry!

4

Soaring

*T*hat same evening, one of the team was playing the piano and singing a little as she led a soaking session.

I decided that during this soaking session I would write a poem, and so I sat down with paper and pen in hand and I tried to write a poem. But I could not. Absolutely nothing came whatsoever. No matter how hard I tried, my mind was a complete blank. I couldn't think of anything to write at all, but I kept on trying, struggling to write something, anything.

Eventually my attention was captured by the piano player's voice and the words she was singing. She was singing out, "Don't strive, just come in to my presence." I felt like the Lord was talking to me and wanted to teach me something, so I put down my pen and stopped doing what I was trying to do. I moved myself to another area of the room and began to rest in God's presence.

Almost immediately, in my mind, I could see a picture of an eagle. As I sat there watching him flying through the valleys and over the mountains, I felt God say to me "Write down words that describe what you see and feel," so I did. I picked my pen back up and began to write a list of words like: eagle, flying, wings, soaring, high up, peaceful, stillness, strength and power. Then I felt like the Lord was saying to me, "Now write a poem from these words." And so the poem *Soaring* began to emerge.

I then felt to add to the poem sentences that didn't come from the picture I was given of the eagle, but which were from the many prophetic words and pictures I had been given from other people earlier in that year. They began rapidly coming back to mind and were all about being in the nest, being tipped out of the nest and being taught to fly.

Again, like the poem *Closer*, this poem reflects the journey I have been on and am still on:

Soaring …

Soaring

$\mathcal{I}$ see a majestic eagle, displaying beauty and grace in flight,
With a flap of His wings He reveals power and might.
He circles towards me and my heart sings,
He calls "soar with me, expand your wings".
I snuggle under His wing as I enter His nest,
There I find protection, there I find rest.
From out of His mouth, me He does nourish,
I begin to grow, I begin to flourish.
He tips me out of the nest to teach me to fly,
Swooping down ready to catch me as I begin to try.
As long as I fly with Him and with Him remain,
Beyond my imagination new heights we attain.
We criss and we cross in an aerial dance,
That speaks of love, that speaks of romance.
As we ride the air currents, going higher and higher,
We are joined in the weave by an angelic choir.
As we intermingle in the heavenly sound,
I lose myself and in Him am found.
A stillness in soaring, a peace so profound,
Only with Christ can this truly be found.
This is amazing, I soar with God's son,
We may be two, but we soar as one.

Wednesday 29th October, 2014

Poetry? But I Don't Do Poetry!

5

Worship

$\mathcal{O}$n the Friday morning of that same week, our time of 24-hour worship began; it commenced at 10am and concluded at 10am the following day. My time slot for leading was to be from 2am to 3am Saturday morning, for which, if you remember, I had signed up for poetry. I stood there looking at my sign-up slot with this word "Poetry" in it and began laughing as I remembered the conversation (okay, disagreement) I had had with the Holy Spirit regarding this idea of His just four days before. Since Monday I had written four poems and was now very much looking forward to what God was going to do in this session.

By the time it came to 2 o'clock in the morning we were all pretty tired and I knew therefore that trying to write poetry could possibly be a challenge for us. So, I looked to the Father and said, "This is your idea, what do you want to do?" I felt that I was given instruction and words to speak over the people in the room. The instruction was to relax and let the Holy Spirit guide us. As I released the words given by the Holy Spirit over the group, the presence of the Lord came, and He brought life to the session and life to the poetry writing.

We wrote for 40 minutes and then spent the last 20 minutes sharing what we had all written. Every person present wrote a poem and I was blown away by what they wrote; their poems were so good.

Because we were doing 24 hours of worship, I had imagined each session would consist of either singing worship songs or praising God or giving thanks. However, during this time I began to understand that worship comes in many forms. Simply sitting down with God and writing a poem together is actually worship and God loves it and so do I.

During the time set aside to write, I just kept thinking about words that I felt described who God was, and is, to me, and from those words came the poem *Worship*.

And so, to *Worship* …

Worship

Creator God, beginning and end,
To you my worship I do send.
For you are Lord, you are King,
You are redeemer of everything.
You are invincible, you are victorious,
You are beautiful, you are glorious.
You are righteous, you are just,
You are faithful, you are trust.
You are gracious, you are good,
You are truthful in your word.
You are great, you are holy,
You truly are the one and only.
You are mercy, you are love,
I send my worship to you above.

Saturday 1ˢᵗ November, 2014

Poetry? But I Don't Do Poetry!

6

Prayer for Cyprus

*E*very week the House of Prayer team hold a time of prayer to intercede for the nation of Cyprus and on this particular Monday it was the turn of my housemates and I to lead.

We had prayed about how to lead the session and felt led to draw a huge outline map of the country on a large sheet of paper that was big enough to cover two tables. We invited people to ask God what the new Cyprus looked like and then encouraged them to write words, scriptures and draw pictures of what they felt they were given on the map and pray it through. We then took the map outside and each shared what we had received and then proclaimed it into the atmosphere for Cyprus.

During the session I wasn't thinking about writing a poem, I was waiting on the Lord for any revelation that I could contribute to the map. I felt I was given a prayer but as I wrote it, it actually came out as a poem.

And so, a prayer, in the form of a poem, for the nation of Cyprus …

Prayer for Cyprus

Jesus, in Cyprus, you are Lord,
Bless this land to be in one accord.
Through this Nation may your living water flow,
Touching people's hearts, setting them aglow.
Release revival, cause an awakening,
Until this whole Nation, your praises sing.
Walk by every person in this land,
Releasing people by the touch of your hand.
Eradicate the darkness with your light,
Come Lord Jesus, hear our plight.
Release your truth throughout this land,
Establish Cyprus to be your Holy Ground.

Monday 3rd November, 2014

Poetry? But I Don't Do Poetry!

7

Lord Jesus, What is it About Your Name?

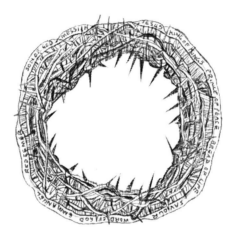

The following day we had our regular time of worship before the commencement of the afternoon session. During the worship, I seemed to lose myself as I began to contemplate the name of Jesus. I remained focused on the name of Jesus and the power that Jesus' name held. As I was lost in this place of contemplation, poetry began to flow, and I simply wrote down all that the Holy Spirit brought to mind.

I didn't have time to complete what had been started, so I left it knowing that I would pick it up again as soon as I had time.

It was the following evening before I returned to writing the poem.

I settled myself down with the hope that I could continue to write the poem, and as I turned my focus once more to the name of Jesus, I felt like the Lord transported me back to the place of worship and contemplation that I had been lost in the day before. Being back in that moment, meditating once again on the name of Jesus, I found that the poetry naturally picked up and continued from where it had been left.

So, this poem comes from my simple contemplation of Jesus' name …

Jesus' Name

Lord Jesus, what is it about your name?
It is unique, no other the same.
It commands authority
Speaks of deity
Eradicates darkness
Demands justice
It holds mighty power
It blossoms a flower
It stands as a fortress
Hearts, it does caress
It protects like a shield
It causes lives to yield
Promises faithful dedication
In souls, brings transformation
It's forgiving and cleansing
Releases mercy, grace and blessing
It heals and restores
Opens heaven's doors
The wonder of your name cannot be explained,
But the love of it leaves us forever changed!

Wednesday November 5th, 2014

Poetry? But I Don't Do Poetry!

8

Do You Know, Long Before the World Began . . .

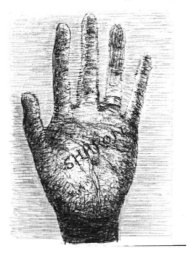

$\mathcal{D}$uring the fifth week of the internship, we had some teaching on the Father Heart of God where we delved into the scriptures that reveal God's love for us.

During one session we were asked to write a letter to Daddy God and to put in it what we would want Him to do for us or who we wanted Him to be to us. Initially I thought that this would be quite a challenge but as soon as I put pen to paper, words and tears began to flow together and they didn't stop for a long time.

Whilst I found the whole exercise extremely moving, releasing and powerful, I knew that the letter I wrote stemmed from things in my past that had hurt me, left me wounded and caused me to put up barriers in certain areas of my life.

Later that night, alone in my room, I opened up my heart to the Lord and began to pour out all the hurts and wounds that I had experienced in the past and desperately wanted to be healed from; all this internal junk just came tumbling out. I guess it needed to. As I lay in bed, I said to Daddy God, "I can't carry all this, please take it, please remove the barriers in our relationship."

Although I had forgiven those that had caused me hurt, what had happened had left scars and insecurities in my life, and this in turn was having an impact on not only truly believing God could really love me, but also from receiving His love for me.

As I went to sleep that night, I truly believed and trusted that from this whole experience I would begin to see transformation in my relationship with God as Father, but I never expected it to begin from the moment I woke up the next morning.

As soon as I awoke, I was reminded by the Holy Spirit about two lines of poetry I had written in my note book at some point during the previous week that didn't seem to belong to anything else, they were …

> *Sharon, you are my child, I hold you in my heart.*
> *My promise is true, we will never be apart.*

I believed that God wanted to say something to me, and as I didn't have class that morning, I took the time to go back over the notes that I had made from the teaching we had received on the Father Heart of God. I also read through the various scriptures we had been given. I read them through slowly and personalised them where I could. As I did so, the words came to life and began to touch my heart; I was hearing and receiving the truth the Lord was whispering to me:

All praise to God, the Father of our Lord Jesus Christ, who has blessed us with every spiritual blessing in the heavenly realms because we are united with Christ. Even before He made the world, God loved us and chose us in Christ to be holy and without fault in His eyes. God decided in advance to adopt us into His own family by bringing us to Himself through Jesus Christ. This is what He wanted to do, and it gave Him great pleasure.

Ephesians 1:3-5

You received God's Spirit when He adopted you as His own children. Now we call Him, "Abba, Father." For His Spirit joins with our spirit to affirm that we are God's children. And since we are His children, we are His heirs.

Romans 8:15-17

I will be your Father and you will be my sons and daughters.

2 Corinthians 6:18

See, I have written your name on the palms of my hands.

Isaiah 49:16

You have captured my heart, my treasure, my bride.

Song of Songs 4:9

Poetry? But I Don't Do Poetry!

See what great love the Father has lavished on us,
that we should be called children of God! And that is
what we are!

1 John 3:1

From the revelation I was receiving in my spirit, a poem began to emerge; very clearly Daddy God wanted to tell me something, and this is what I felt He had to say …

Do You Know?

Do you know, long before the world began,
I loved you, I chose you, you were in my plan?
I looked into the future and I could clearly see
That my kingdom would be incomplete if you weren't here
with me.

Do you know I designed you, thought about every part?
As you began to be formed I was rejoicing in my heart.
I watched as you were born and from your first cry out loud
I boasted about you to all of heaven, I couldn't have been
more proud.

Do you know I watched over you each and every day as you
grew?
I couldn't wait for that moment when of my love for you,
you knew.
I needed you to love me, so patiently I did stand
Until you could clearly see your name written upon my
hand.

Do you know I've adopted you, you personally belong to
me?
It fills me with great pleasure when you call my name
"daddy".
You've captivated my heart, you're perfect without flaws,
Just ask of me my precious child, all I have is yours.

Do you know you fill me with joy and over you I sing?
You are beautiful my darling, to me you are everything.
Sharon, you are my child, I hold you within my heart.
My promise to you is true Sharon, we will never be apart.

Poetry? But I Don't Do Poetry!

Do you know I cannot hurt you and I cannot walk away?
I am a good Father, I cannot lie in what I say.
If you didn't know all these truths, you certainly do know
now
I bless you to grasp them in your heart and simply respond
"wow"!

Friday 7ᵗʰ November, 2014

9

Digging Wells

After returning from Cyprus I was wondering in which direction God would lead me next on our journey together, and would it include any more poetry?

God already had a plan sorted and delivered it to me through my friend, Andrea Filgate. Andrea was going around and encouraging people to read their Bibles; in this she set me a challenge: to read the Bible through following a one-year reading plan. It was in that very moment that I had the most incredible revelation: I was no longer afraid to read! My fear of words and the inability to comprehend were gone! God had delivered me from the very foundation of the lie I had always believed so very strongly. I was now free to read the Bible, and I absolutely knew it. It wasn't that I was suddenly brighter and more capable of understanding than before, but that I was no longer dominated by thoughts that I could not. I came to see that this was not a challenge just to read the Bible, but it was in fact an invitation from God Himself to come and meet Him through His Living Word and I was free to do it and was super excited for it.

So, I was literally just nine days into reading my Bible and my reading for the day included Genesis 26. I got caught up on verses 17 to 33. The Holy Spirit was drawing me in. The passage tells the story of Isaac reopening the wells that his father Abraham had dug, about his men digging new wells and about how some of those wells were taken from them. I read the passage through several times and was excited by it. In that moment I believe God was sharing with me that the wells symbolised the scriptures and the digging was about reading them to find fresh and living water and that I needed to persist in my digging/reading and not to become discouraged, even if I found it hard and frustrating at times.

I felt so blessed to be encouraged in such a way by God. But apparently, as far as God was concerned, that was not enough encouragement; He wanted to give more.

In the early hours of the next morning, about 2am, I suddenly woke up to find a poem emerging from the same passage in Genesis. I was ever so sleepy, so I said to God, "If You want me to write a poem right now, then you are going to have to wake me up because I am way too tired". Within five seconds flat my whole being was wide-awake, and I mean wide awake. So, I got up, crept downstairs, grabbed pen, paper and

Bible, shut myself in our front room, got all cosy and began to write.

I started with writing down the poetry lines I had woken up with, and built on them from there, using for inspiration what God had revealed to me earlier through the Bible passage. I then read the same verses repeatedly, asking the Holy Spirit each time to reveal more, and trusted that He was leading me as I continued to write.

After a couple of hours, the poem *Digging Wells* was written, and I was satisfied with it, so I went back to bed. Getting into bed, I just quickly asked God if there was anything else He wanted to add to the poem or reveal to me about it before I went back to sleep. I didn't expect anything, as I thought the poem was complete but straightaway, in my mind, I could see a picture. In the picture God showed me something from my childhood. First, He reminded me how we used to get milk delivered; it was delivered in glass bottles with a silver foil sealed top. Then He went on to show me how birds used to peck through the foil top and just take the cream from the surface of the milk. I knew what the Lord was saying but I was now more than ready to go to sleep, so I asked the Holy Spirit to remind me of it in the morning, which He faithfully did. From this picture I added verse 3 to the poem about not just drinking from the surface.

And so to *Digging Wells* ...

Digging Wells

Though we stand in Christ on solid ground,
We need to dig beneath if treasure is to be found.
Fresh water lies below,
How deep is this eternal flow.

Break up the surface of the living Word,
Seek to find truth to things you have heard.
Dig with the Holy Spirit until fresh and living water is
found,
This will refresh and sustain you as you dig again into
deeper ground.

When you dig, find water and begin to sup,
Don't just drink from the surface and then give up.
Immerse yourself completely and then you will begin to see,
All that your Heavenly Father wishes to reveal to thee.

As you successfully dig, the enemy may rise up to steal,
Depend on Jesus to crush the serpent's head as he tries to
bite your heel.
So you may be hindered or lack motivation,
But keep on persevering, digging wells requires dedication.

Drink deeply from each well and keep on worshipping the
Lord,
God is with you; endless blessings and success are assured.
You see, God made a promise of the unbreakable kind,
Seek, yes seek me, and you will surely find.

Digging Wells

As you dig new wells and discover fresh water anew,
You will come across abandoned ones, they are important too.
Re-open these wells, clear out the rubble,
Take a fresh look; it will be worth the trouble.

Old wells can spring forth life as well as the new,
You will be fed and encouraged between the two.
As you dig discovering and re-discovering truths both ancient and new,
Rely on the strength, direction and love of God who holds the shovel with you.

January 10th, 2015

Poetry? But I Don't Do Poetry!

10

Bread and Wine

This next poem took me on a journey that lasted about 18 months and it all started with two lines:

As we drink the wine and eat the bread unleavened,
We are to remember Christ, now seated in heaven.

These two lines were all I had, and they just kept going around in my head and I didn't know what to do with them. I sought God on them but still nothing came to mind, so I made a note of them and then just left them to one side.

A few weeks later we had a guest speaker in church, Rob Ash (a singer/songwriter), who throughout the evening sang a number of songs that he had composed. As he sang, it was like I was hearing for the very first time, poetry being sung, and I was mesmerised.

After the service I chatted with Rob and asked him some questions about where he got his inspiration from, and how he went about writing his songs etc. I shared the two lines of poetry I had with him and asked his advice on what to do with them. He shared with me what he did when this happened to him and then told me to go and do likewise. Rob's advice was simple, it was to go and look in the Bible and find out all that I could from the words in the poetry lines and then take all my notes from that study and write a poem or song from them.

I now knew what God was wanting me to do with the two lines of poetry. Unlike the last poem where God gave me a portion of scripture to write from, this time I felt God wanted me to search the scriptures with Him to find the poem. This was different and I did instinctively what came to mind, which was to explore the gospels.

Asking the Holy Spirit for revelation, I read through Matthew 26-28, Mark 14-16, Luke 22-24 and John 13-20. As I read, re-read and pondered on each chapter, I wrote down everything that Jesus was subjected to through the last hours of His life. As I began to put the four accounts together side by side, I was amazed by how much bigger a picture was being revealed. I had never done this kind of Bible study before.

Inspired by the Holy Spirit, I then began to draw from my notes the terrible ordeal Jesus suffered, writing them in poetic form as I went.

I came to a place where I was happy with what was written and considered the poem complete, and therefore put it away in my poetry folder, where it stayed until June of the following year.

Then one Sunday morning our Pastor, Rhiannon Thomas, spoke on the seven ways in which Jesus' blood was spilt. It was a superb and fascinating teaching and I was busy enjoying it, when suddenly out of the blue, all I could think about was this poem that I had written over a year before. I was asking myself "had I mentioned all the ways in which Jesus bled in my poem or not?" I knew for certain that one way was definitely missing. I asked Rhiannon about it and she directed me to Isaiah 50, 52 and 53.

Following the same process that I had the year before, I read through the chapters in Isaiah a few times and wrote down notes from all that was revealed to me. From this new Bible study, more lines were added to the poem. Rhiannon read the poem and challenged me to go deeper still, so I asked the Holy Spirit to show me more and as He did so the poem continued to grow, until it was finally complete.

Here I share with you what I discovered about some of Christ's journey …

Bread and Wine

As we drink the wine and eat the bread unleavened,
We are to remember Christ, now seated in heaven.

Take a moment to ponder on Christ's horrific journey,
What He went through before He gave up His life so freely.
Jesus knew the scriptures, how His death was by prophets foretold,
But still He rode into Jerusalem so the future plan would uphold.
The crowds who were cheering, "Hosanna, praise the Lord",
Would soon turn to shouting, "Crucify Him, He's a fraud".
In Gethsemane, His soul crushed with grief, Jesus was uttering,
"Abba Father, your will, not mine" and so drank the cup of suffering.
Through agony of spirit, sweat drops of blood fell from His brow,
He knew His purpose; He knew the time was now.
Betrayed for 30 pieces of silver and by a disciple's kiss,
He was also denied by a friend who had vowed would never do this.
An army of angels for protection He could have called forth hence,
But He did not; He chose to walk in complete obedience.
To questions and false accusations spoken, lie after lie,
Through all this He remained silent, He gave no reply.
An innocent man, found guilty and convicted,
As a false prophet and blasphemer, He was depicted.
To a criminal's death on a cross He was sentenced,
The onslaught of incredible torture commenced.
They clothed Him with a purple robe and verbally they began to abuse,

Mockingly they saluted, worshipped and hailed Him "King
of the Jews".
He was blindfolded, bound and beaten for amusement,
They ridiculed Him and cruel insults were vent.
He was spat on and slapped across the face,
He was despised and taunted by the human race.
He was stripped of His clothing, leaving Him shamed and
exposed,
Taking a reed stick to His head, He was beaten by His foes.
Grabbing hold of His beard, whiskers were ripped from His
chin,
All this and more was done to a man without sin.
With force, a crown of thorns was pushed onto His head,
He was ripped to shreds by a whip tipped with spiked lead.
To torture within an inch of death was Roman tradition,
This severe beating left Jesus' face beyond recognition.
Upon His scourged body, Jesus picked up and carried the
weight of the cross,
To express with words such extreme anguish, I am
completely at a loss.
Like a lamb led to the slaughter,
He walked on for every son and every daughter.
They drove the nails through His hands, and through His
feet,
Then by casting lots for His clothes, they did compete.
Whilst nailed to the cross He was still subjected to
humiliation,
Because of unbelief, because of rejection.
A sign "The King of the Jews" was pinned above His head,
The accusers failed to see the truth in what it actually said.
Beseeching His Father for mercy, for me and for you,
Jesus cried out "Father, forgive them, they know not what
they do".
From the Son with whom He was well pleased, God turned
His face,

He withheld His almighty power to allow the sacrifice to
take place.
Jesus knew His Father had turned away, He felt the agony of
isolation,
But His goal was to complete the sacrifice in order to secure
redemption.
Into His Father's hands, Jesus, His Spirit, He freely
released,
"It is finished" was His last cry, the perfect sacrifice
complete.
Thrusting a spear, they pierced His side,
Blood and water flowed out, His death certified.
Darkness fell across the land, the earth rumbled,
The curtain was torn in two, the stone temple crumbled.
Buried in a tomb that was not His own,
He was sealed in darkness, all alone.

But the grave could not hold Him, so Holy is He,
Sin and death defeated, He rose in victory.

The prophecy spoken long ago needed to be fulfilled,
To confirm the new covenant, Jesus' blood needed to be
spilled.
His blood was poured out so that our sins may be forgiven,
His body broken, that we may receive healing from heaven.
On the spotless sacrificial Lamb our punishment was lain,
We can now stand before God because Christ, our risen
Saviour, was slain.

Jesus said, "Remember me", so let us embrace what has
been given,
As we partake of the wine and of the bread unleavened.

First written February 10th, 2015; Extended July 26th, 2016

11

The Bridegroom and His Bride

$\mathcal{T}$o cut a long story short – Clare Bell, who is a very good friend of mine, meets this guy called Stuart, he proposes, she says yes, we have a match made in heaven.

Clare rings me and asks if I would be willing to write a poem for the wedding. Knowing from experience that I don't just sit down and write a poem, I started asking God, "Please can I write a poem for Clare and Stuart, please will you give me a poem for them, please will you help me write one?"

For quite a while I had nothing, but I persisted in prayer and then one day my daily reading led me through Ecclesiastes 4. As I read verses 9 to 12, I began to get all excited because I knew that something was coming together.

It reads:

> *Two people are better off than one, for they can help each other succeed. If one person falls, the other can reach out and help. But someone who falls alone is in real trouble. Likewise, two people lying close together can keep each other warm. But how can one be warm alone? A person standing alone can be attacked and defeated, but two can stand back-to-back and conquer. Three are even better, for a triple-braided cord is not easily broken.*

From these verses I began to write the poem, adding to it scriptural truths that came to mind from other passages in the Bible.

However, there was one other thing that I really wanted to include in the poem. I absolutely love the whole concept of speaking God-given words of blessing over people and I didn't want to miss this opportunity. So, I asked God if this could be incorporated in the poem so that I could pronounce words of blessings over my friends and their marriage.

To write the blessing part of the poem I read through Numbers 6:22-27 and then asked the Holy Spirit to reveal the words that He would like to bless Stuart and Clare with. I wrote down all the words I felt He gave me and crafted them into rhyming lines of blessings. Not something I had done before but thoroughly enjoyed doing.

Completed just in time for the wedding day: *The Bridegroom and His Bride ...*

The Bridegroom and His Bride

First you are betrothed to your Lord and Saviour,
Secondly, Stuart and Clare, you are married to each other.
God's first commandment is that you love Him above any other,
His second command is that you love one another.

Keep the Father's order and obey His command,
And He will be the solid rock upon which your marriage stands.
Marriage is a precious gift that comes from the Lord,
Making Christ the centre gives the strength of a three-fold cord.

So, cherish this precious gift that has been given to you,
Prayerfully invest in every area and in all that you do.
Just as each day your Father gives you your daily bread,
So be there for each other now you are wed.

So, in the name of Jesus, I bless you Clare and Stu,
May the blessings in your marriage be far from few.
I bless you in your marriage to be so strong together,
That with the help of the Lord, any storm you will weather.

I bless you with abundant love, so you have plenty to give,
I bless your finances that you will have plenty to live.
I bless you with success and favour on all that you do,
And that worship and praise to God will flow naturally from you.

Poetry? But I Don't Do Poetry!

I bless you with a friendship that runs deep and true,
I bless you that communication will flow easily between
you,
I bless you to speak words of encouragement and support,
And that together you will spend time in your Father's
court.

I bless you that your path together will be an easy one,
I bless you that your journey will be filled with laughter and
fun,
I bless you as you travel forth hand in hand, with unity,
And that the Father's joy and peace will continually flood
thee.

I bless you with receiving outrageous grace,
I bless you with deeper revelation of your Father's heart and
face,
In the name of Jesus, Stuart and Clare I bless you two,
So that the Father may pour out His blessings endlessly
upon you.

Amen

April 25ᵗʰ, 2015

12

Mum's Home

"Sharon"

You just know don't you, somewhere deep down inside, when someone says your name in full and in a certain way and says nothing afterwards, that you have to stop what you are doing and face that person and give them your full attention.

It was Tuesday August 4th, 2015, about 6pm, and I was busy in the kitchen preparing food when Lloyd, my husband, came in behind me and said my name. I stopped what I was doing and turned to face him and waited.

"Sharon, I'm so sorry, your mum has died."

"My mum has died? My mum, not your mum, but my mum?" I wanted to make sure.

"Yes, Sharon, your mum, Elaine, has died."

Silent tears began to roll down my cheeks as I began to mentally process this information. I didn't want to believe this totally unexpected announcement, but I had to. I was in a state of shock and disbelief for a few minutes when all of a sudden, out of nowhere, I burst into praise, I couldn't help myself, it seemed so natural.

"Thank you God that she is with You. Thank you God that You gave me the privilege of leading her to You only 15 months ago. Thank you that she was definitely saved. Thank you therefore that the only place she can be right now is with You. Oh my God, thank you, thank you, thank you."

I had an incredible sense of peace deep within me; it was to such an extent that I could honestly say, "It is well with my soul." But at the same time great big deep sobs of grief began to break forth and Lloyd pulled me in close and just held me.

That night our daughter Bethany, Lloyd and I all went to bed as usual and whilst the others slept, I could not. I lay there wide-awake. I seemed to spend my time travelling around in circles with my emotions; I went from shock to disbelief to crying silent tears to praising God. I travelled round this circle for many hours until about 2 o'clock in the morning when my thoughts were interrupted by two words; "Mum's home". I became very still and listened and then there they were again – a tiny whisper "Mum's home". My response was completely automatic, "put the kettle on".

Living three hours' drive away, whenever mum arrived for a stay, I would actually switch the kettle on before walking outside to greet her, knowing that her first sentence on getting out of the car would be, "Hello love, stick the kettle on, I'm gasping for a coffee".

The whisper came again, "Mum's home" and again I responded, "put the kettle on". This cycle of whispered words and my response continued for a little while until it extended. "Mum's home." "Put the kettle on." "No longer to be said now that she is gone!"

A poem? I couldn't believe it. A poem! I wanted to engage so I whispered back to the Lord. "Do You want me to write a poem?" I was both moved and somewhat taken aback as it dawned on me what God wanted to do in that moment. I got out of bed and headed downstairs, grabbed my poetry book and pen and sat down in the front room. From out of my heart I spoke into the stillness of the night, "Lord, my mum has just died, I am in a state of shock and grief, I'm really not able to focus on anything right now but I believe that you want us to write a poem together, so please can you write it through me and for me because there is no way I can do this."

I wrote down the two lines I had, and I really don't know how the rest of it came to be. I can only say that it was totally Holy Spirit led. I know that I worked on the poem for over three hours, but cannot remember or say how it was done, it just was.

It was approaching 6 o'clock in the morning by the time I returned to bed and I instantly fell asleep. Lloyd and Bethany got up in the morning and went to work, as we had agreed, because I knew I would want to spend the day by myself. By the time I woke up the house was quiet, and I went down to the front room and picked up the poem and began to read it.

As I did so, tears flowed down my face, I could not believe what was written, it was so beautiful, so comforting, so profound, so God.

I must have read the poem at least 20 times during that day and each time I would get caught up in a different line and would weep again. When Lloyd and Bethany came home, I shared the poem with them, and they stood there in utter disbelief. Lloyd asked me at least three times, "Did you write this poem?" They were both very moved by the words. In awe of what God had done, Lloyd eventually said, "Wow Sharon, God really loves you, doesn't He? He has written this for you, hasn't He? That's amazing love."

At my mum's flat a few days later, I noticed her Christian calendar was next to her bed. I had bought it for her the previous Christmas, and it had a word for each day on it. Though she had died peacefully in her sleep from a heart attack at some time during the night, we don't know exactly what time, she had turned the calendar to 4th August, the date she entered heaven, and the first three words read, "Hold my hand". You will see it in the eighth line of the poem too.

I knew writing this chapter was going to be hard for me and indeed I have cried the whole way through typing it, but I also knew that I wanted to share the story because it also brings me much joy, it gladdens my heart to know where my mum is and it reminds me how loved I am and how good God is. I am still in awe as I think back to how God, in His love, grace and mercy, cut through my grief with a poem that opened my eyes to see the most beautiful scene that in turn helped me greatly in the grieving and healing process.

It is said that a picture paints a thousand words, but in this case, a few words paints the most glorious picture …

Mum's Home

Mum's home, put the kettle on!
No longer to be said now that she is gone.
She breathed her last and closed her eyes,
The immediate touch took her by surprise.
She looked and saw true love shining on His face,
And realised He was Jesus as she was held in His embrace.
"Elaine" He whispered, "your journey has finished here below,
So come my child, take my hand, it's time to go."
Enveloped in peace and crowned with love,
She left this world for heaven above.
At heaven's gates mum arrived,
Jesus never left her side.
He threw wide open the pearly gate,
"Come on" He said, "they just can't wait."
She entered in and there beheld,
Angels and loved ones and God unveiled.
And they were singing in joyful tones,
"Hallelujah, hallelujah, Elaine is home."

Wednesday August 5th, 2015

Poetry? But I Don't Do Poetry!

13

The Complete Gospel

$\mathcal{I}$n March 2016 I found myself back in The House of Prayer in Cyprus, only this time Lloyd was with me. I was so excited being with Lloyd in the place where I had had such an amazing time with God and such an incredible breakthrough that it had altered, and was continuing to alter, my life. We went to Cyprus to have a little break and also to attend a four-day conference organised by Martin and Heike.

The teaching was based on the fullness of the Gospel: Incarnation, Crucifixion, Resurrection, Ascension and Pentecost, not only what that looked like for Jesus but also what it looks like for us today. It was about walking in the fullness of the complete Gospel so we can grow to be mature Christians.

The teaching was excellent, I really enjoyed it, and this time I was fully free from problems in understanding. However, whether we are struggling or not, there are times when God really wants us to grasp something, so He goes that extra mile to reveal things to us. This ensures that whatever it is that He is teaching us in that moment, the revelation is such that it becomes deeply embedded within us.

This is what I believe God wanted to do with me with this teaching. I woke up about 5am and just absolutely knew that God wanted me to write a poem based on the teaching we were receiving. There were no beginning lines to the poem, no downloads, just a clear prompting to get up and write.

So up I got and sat at the table with my notes from the conference and asked the Holy Spirit for help. I pored over the notes that I had taken, reading them through several times. From within them a poem began to surface, and I wrote quickly. It didn't take very long, about two hours, but I felt that the poem brought together all the teaching that we had received in a kind of summary.

So here is what I felt the Father really wanted me to grasp from the teaching …

The Complete Gospel

In the beginning God, it is stated,
The heavens and earth and all things He created.
He spoke the Word; life formed and began to thrive,
Into man He breathed His fullness, Adam was alive.

For a time, heaven and earth were one with each other,
God and man walked in perfect harmony together.
Then came the great fall, sin was committed,
Heaven's gate was slammed shut, man no longer admitted.

But it wasn't just heaven and earth where there was a great
divide,
In mind, emotions and spirit, man was torn inside.
Our spirit was depleted, it shrivelled and died,
Were we better off? No! Satan had lied.

We were now apart from our Father here on earth,
We lost our identity, our authority, our unity, our worth.
It broke the Father's heart to see His children lost,
He longed for restored relationship and was willing to pay
the cost.

Incarnation:

From out of His heart, God sent His Son,
Word became flesh, God and man in one.
Jesus was fully Son of God, fully Son of Man,
Restoration was His goal, His purpose, His plan.

Poetry? But I Don't Do Poetry!

Crucifixion and Resurrection:

Jesus walked on earth to show the way,
Then on the cross His life down, He chose to lay.
His Spirit couldn't die; it went to hell to retrieve what was lost,
The gateway to heaven was re-opened because He settled sin's cost.

Ascension and Pentecost:

Christ arose; body and spirit were re-united,
We are now seated with Him, God is delighted.
The work was completed and for those who believe,
The fullness of God, through the Holy Spirit, are free to receive.

Incarnation, Crucifixion, Resurrection, Ascension and Pentecost,
Without this complete Gospel, our spirits, in part, can still be lost.
We were designed to be fully man with fully God indwelling,
So soak your spirit with the full Gospel so you can walk fully living.

Friday 18th March, 2016

14

Commit

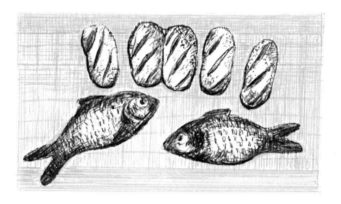

$\mathcal{T}$his poem came about very much like the second poem I wrote entitled *Behold*.

This time I had the word "commit" going around and around in my head. This word kept popping up everywhere and I knew that God was trying to teach/tell me something important, but I wasn't really getting it.

As I was reading the Bible, two separate verses really caught my attention as I came across them. They both contained the word "commit". I kept reading them over and over.

Poetry? But I Don't Do Poetry!

Commit your actions to the Lord, and your plans will succeed.

Proverbs 16:3

Commit everything you do to the Lord. Trust Him, and He will help you.

Psalm 37:5

I kept asking God, "What does this look like for me? What does it really mean? What are You asking me to do?"

As I continued to ask these questions and meditate on the two verses the Holy Spirit began to release revelation from the Father's heart regarding the word "commit". It came quite simply and easily and flowed naturally into a poem. Again, it took very little effort on my part. It was more like the Holy Spirit sharing an important instruction, explaining it clearly for me as He did so through poetry.

So here is what the Lord had to say to me about the word "commit" …

Commit

Commit – "Father," I ask, "what does that look like? What should I do?"

He responds, "Invite me into your daily life, I want to engage with you.

Stop looking at yourself, turn your eyes towards me,
Lay down your plans entirely and then just let them be.
When you surrender them to me and allow me to lead,
Your plans will come to life as into them I breathe.
As you commit to me, we merge into one,
Only then do we journey forward as father and son.
Listen attentively as I guide you in what to do,
Your plans spring to life as you follow my instruction through.
Keep asking me for help with each and every step of the way,
I want to be involved in the little and big things throughout your day.
Allow me freedom to take some plans away,
And trust me completely as, on your heart, new plans I lay.
In my hands your plans get off the ground,
In my hands your plans will abound.
I will open every door for you and every need provide,
As you partner with Holy Spirit, our interaction stays alive.
I have the power for I am the Lion and the Lamb,
I am your Father, the great I AM.
My promise is true, in my hands your plans will succeed,
As you commit your actions to me, they will succeed indeed."

Monday 20th February, 2017

Poetry? But I Don't Do Poetry!

The Fruit

Through this creative journey, God has broken off the chains of captivity, healed me, inspired me, taught me, encouraged me and given me the gift of writing poetry. God, in His grace and mercy, removed a foundational lie and replaced it with His truth in such an extraordinary and creative way that it has left me in awe of His goodness. I now absolutely know deep within my heart that God is the source of my wisdom, knowledge and understanding.

As I began to read the Bible, a passion within me began to grow to get to know God more and more. I have found that when I rely on the Holy Spirit, by partnering with Him as I read, He opens up the Word and reveals His truth in it. I am so completely and utterly free to read that I no longer worry if I don't understand some chapters of the Bible when I read it, it doesn't put me off or stop me. I know if I need to understand something then the Holy Spirit will give me revelation.

Poetry? But I Don't Do Poetry!

I have found a real joy in being in God's Word each day and I can't wait to see what will unfold. I am always excited for my next encounter with God, what I will hear Him say, what He will reveal to me about Himself, what He will teach me and share with me. God just keeps drawing me into Himself and I can't help but go.

My now closer, more intimate relationship with God is the best fruit of this whole adventure. God has been so gracious and merciful towards me, He came and met me in my need when I didn't even ask Him to, which shows just how good and how loving God is. I can only give God all the glory, as it all belongs to Him.

In the name of Jesus, may God bless you with greater revelation of who He is and of His love for you and may you grow in creativity as you journey with Him.

My heart has heard you say,
"Come and talk with me."
And my heart responds,
"Lord I am coming."
Psalm 27:8

My child, pay attention to what I say.
Listen carefully to my words.
Don't lose sight of them.
Let them penetrate deep into your heart,
for they bring life to those who find them,
and healing to their whole body.
Proverbs 4:20-22

Amen

Information

Closer Internship:

My time on the "Closer" Internship was for me six weeks that totally transformed my life and relationship with God. I am so grateful to Martin and Heike for their love for and obedience to God, for their love for people and for the commitment and sacrifices they, and their whole team, make to run this internship. For more information about the Living Stones House of Prayer in Cyprus and the Closer Internship that they run, please visit their website at www.hopcyprus.org.

CD Recording:

There is a CD included with this book on which you will find all the poems for those who prefer to listen to them rather than read. You will also find a specially recorded Holy Spirit led soaking session for your enjoyment.

Clare Bell:

Clare is an especially gifted and anointed worship leader, playing not only guitar, piano and flute, she also has the most beautiful and powerful singing voice. She is very much led by the Holy Spirit as she leads worship and I usually find myself caught up in this worship and landing in the throne room to spend time with God. Clare was therefore my only choice as to who would do the music for the CD accompanying this book. And because she is such a great friend, she readily agreed.

Clare has recorded a couple of albums and they are amazing. I would greatly encourage you to treat yourself to a copy. Clare's album *One Take Worship:With Worship We Come* has original songs written by Clare and has a Celtic feel and sound to it – the songs are both beautiful and powerful. The second is a Christmas album called *A Celtic Christmas* which releases incredible peace as it is played – I love it.

You can purchase her music on *iTunes*.
Clare also runs workshops in worship and prophetic song for congregations and worship teams.

You can visit Clare's website at: www.clarebellworship.com

Book Purchase and Contact Information:

If you wish to purchase further copies of this book, or Clare's Christmas album, you will find them available on Etsy through my daughter's shop called *Treasured Creativity*: www.etsy.com/uk/shop/treasuredcreativity.

Alternatively, you can email me at:
sharon.george3@btinternet.com